contents

When fresh, fish will smell fishy (though not bad) and be springy to the touch. Whole fish should have bright eyes and shiny, slippery skin. Buy molluscs and crustaceans either alive or cooked, and discard any clams, mussels or pipis that do not close when tapped sharply. Eat responsibly and choose fish that are farmed in a sustainable way; your fishmonger will advise you.

At home, store seafood in the refrigerator, loosely covered in foil and eat as soon as possible. Purge clams, cockles and pipis of sand before cooking them by placing in cold, salted water for an hour. Kill live crustaceans as humanely as possible by freezing them for at least 2 hours before cooking.

Seafood tips

Nature's fast food is delicate and delicious – the perfect summer food. It is the after-work chef's secret weapon: easy to prepare and the basis for some fast-cooking, great-tasting meals.

In summer, barbecuing and grilling seafood are the simplest ways to prepare it. Cook over medium heat and remove as soon as the flesh has turned opaque – it will continue to cook when removed from the heat. For whole fish, slash each side twice and use a greased fish-shaped hinged grill to make turning the fish easy. It is cooked when a skewer slides easily into the thickest part.

For foolproof fish, enclose fillets in an aluminium foil parcel and place onto the grill or barbecue. The gentle steaming will infuse the fish with the flavour of any other ingredients you've included, and will produce melt-in-your-mouth results.

Boil or steam molluscs with a little wine or stock for flavour; discard any that do not open. Crustaceans can simply be dropped into boiling water, they are done once they have changed colour.

seafood antipasto

12 uncooked large king prawns
  (840g)
8 sardine fillets (360g)
8 whole cleaned baby octopus
  (720g)
2 cloves garlic, crushed
2 tablespoons olive oil
440g loaf ciabatta bread,
  sliced thickly
170g asparagus, halved
  lengthways
200g grape tomatoes
1 cup (150g) seeded
  kalamata olives
250g haloumi cheese, sliced
  lengthways into 8 pieces
garlic chilli dressing
4 cloves garlic, crushed
1 tablespoon finely grated
  lime rind
¼ cup (60ml) lime juice
2 fresh small red thai chillies,
  chopped finely

1 Make garlic chilli dressing.
2 Shell and devein prawns, leaving heads
and tails intact. Combine prawns in large
bowl with sardines, octopus, half the garlic
and half the oil. Cover; refrigerate 3 hours
or overnight.
3 Combine remaining garlic and oil in small
bowl; brush bread slices, both sides, with
garlic oil. Toast bread, both sides, on heated
oiled barbecue flat plate.
4 Cook asparagus, tomatoes, olives and
cheese, in batches, on barbecue flat plate,
until vegetables are tender and cheese is
browned lightly.
5 Cook seafood, in batches, on barbecue
flat plate until cooked as desired; drizzle with
dressing. Serve with vegetables and cheese.
garlic chilli dressing Combine ingredients
in screw-top jar; shake well.

preparation time 25 minutes
(plus refrigeration time)
cooking time 20 minutes
serves 4
nutritional count per serving 51.1g total fat
(15.4g saturated fat); 4840kJ (1158 cal);
63.2g carbohydrate; 108g protein; 6.2g fibre

salt and pepper salmon with wasabi mayonnaise

2 teaspoons sea salt
2 teaspoons sichuan pepper
¼ cup (60ml) vegetable oil
4 x 220g salmon fillets, skin on
wasabi mayonnaise
½ cup (150g) mayonnaise
2 teaspoons wasabi paste
1 teaspoon finely chopped fresh coriander
1 teaspoon lime juice

1 Using mortar and pestle, crush salt and pepper until fine. Combine pepper mixture, half the oil and fish in large bowl; cover, stand 5 minutes.
2 Meanwhile, make wasabi mayonnaise.
3 Heat remaining oil in large frying pan; cook fish, skin-side down, until skin crisps. Turn fish; cook, uncovered, until cooked as desired. Serve fish with wasabi mayonnaise, and watercress and lime slices, if desired.
wasabi mayonnaise Combine ingredients in small bowl.

preparation time 10 minutes
cooking time 15 minutes
serves 4
nutritional count per serving 40.1g total fat (6.3g saturated fat); 2278kJ (545 cal); 7.5g carbohydrate; 39.4 protein; 0.2g fibre

salmon en papillote

Cooking something en papillote means it is encased in baking paper or foil, so that it cooks by steaming in its own juices. In this recipe, any oily fish can be used, as long as the fillets are of equal size and thickness.

1 medium tomato (150g), seeded, chopped finely
1 tablespoon rinsed, drained baby capers
1 small red onion (100g), chopped finely
2 teaspoons finely grated lemon rind
4 x 220g salmon fillets
1 tablespoon lemon juice
1 tablespoon olive oil
80g baby rocket leaves
2 tablespoons finely shredded fresh basil

1 Preheat oven to 200°C/180°C fan-forced.
2 Combine tomato, capers, onion and rind in small bowl.
3 Place each fillet, skin-side down, on large square of oiled foil. Top each fillet with equal amounts of tomato mixture. Gather corners of foil together above fish; twist to enclose securely.
4 Place parcels on oven tray; bake about 10 minutes or until fish is cooked as desired.
5 Combine lemon juice and oil in small jug. Divide rocket among serving plates.
6 Unwrap parcels just before serving; place fish on rocket. Top with basil, drizzle with oil mixture.

preparation time 15 minutes
cooking time 10 minutes
serves 4
nutritional count per serving 19g total fat (3.8g saturated fat); 11434kJ (343 cal); 2.6g carbohydrate; 40.1g protein; 1g fibre

seared salmon kerala-style with lime pickle yogurt

2 teaspoons coriander seeds
1 teaspoon cumin seeds
2 cardamom pods, bruised
1 cinnamon stick
1 teaspoon ground turmeric
½ teaspoon chilli powder
2 tablespoons peanut oil
2 cloves garlic, crushed
4 x 265g salmon cutlets
100g baby spinach leaves
lime pickle yogurt
½ cup (140g) yogurt
2 tablespoons lime pickle, chopped finely

1 Dry-fry coriander, cumin, cardamom and cinnamon in small heated frying pan over medium heat, stirring, until fragrant. Stir in turmeric and chilli powder; remove from heat.
2 Using mortar and pestle, crush spices until ground finely; transfer to large bowl. Stir in oil and garlic; add fish, turn fish to coat in mixture. Cover; refrigerate 30 minutes.
3 Meanwhile, make lime pickle yogurt.
4 Cook fish in heated oiled grill pan. Serve fish with spinach and yogurt.
lime pickle yogurt Combine ingredients in small bowl.

preparation time 20 minutes
(plus refrigeration time)
cooking time 15 minutes
serves 4
nutritional count per serving 29.3g total fat (6.7g saturated fat); 2082kJ (498 cal); 3.9g carbohydrate; 54.1g protein; 1.1g fibre
note Lime pickle is an Indian special mixed pickle/condiment of limes that adds a hot and spicy taste to meals, especially rice. Available from Indian food shops.

11

grilled salmon with nam jim and herb salad

4 x 220g salmon fillets,
   skin on
nam jim
3 long green chillies,
   chopped coarsely
2 fresh small red thai chillies,
   chopped coarsely
2 cloves garlic, quartered
1 shallot (25g), quartered
2cm piece fresh ginger (10g),
   quartered
⅓ cup (80ml) lime juice
2 tablespoons fish sauce
1 tablespoon grated
   palm sugar
1 tablespoon peanut oil
¼ cup (40g) roasted unsalted
   cashews, chopped finely
herb salad
1½ cups loosely packed
   fresh mint leaves
1 cup loosely packed
   fresh coriander leaves
1 cup loosely packed
   fresh basil leaves, torn
1 medium red onion (170g),
   sliced thinly
2 lebanese cucumbers (260g),
   seeded, sliced thinly

1 Make nam jim.
2 Cook salmon, both sides, on heated oiled grill plate (or grill or barbecue) until cooked as desired.
3 Meanwhile, combine ingredients for herb salad in medium bowl.
4 Serve salmon and herb salad topped with nam jim.

nam jim Blend or process chillies, garlic, shallot, ginger, juice, sauce, sugar and oil until smooth; stir in nuts.

preparation time 30 minutes
cooking time 10 minutes
serves 4
nutritional count per serving 25g total fat (5.1g saturated fat); 1948kJ (466 cal); 10.8g carbohydrate; 47.6g protein; 4.4g fibre
note Nam jim is a generic term for a Thai dipping sauce; most versions include fish sauce and chillies, but the remaining ingredients are up to the cook's discretion.

angel hair pasta with smoked salmon and asparagus

375g angel hair pasta
¼ cup (60ml) olive oil
250g asparagus, trimmed,
chopped coarsely
150g smoked salmon,
sliced thinly
2 tablespoons rinsed, drained
baby capers
⅓ cup finely chopped
fresh chives
75g baby rocket leaves
1 lemon, cut into wedges

1 Cook pasta in large saucepan of boiling water, uncovered, until just tender.
2 Meanwhile, heat oil in small frying pan; cook asparagus, stirring, until tender.
3 Drain pasta; return pasta to pan with salmon, capers, asparagus, chives and rocket; toss to combine. Serve pasta with lemon.

preparation time 10 minutes
cooking time 10 minutes
serves 4
nutritional count per serving 16.6g total fat (2.5g saturated fat); 2128kJ (509 cal); 66g carbohydrate; 20.9g protein; 4.7g fibre
note Also known as capelli d'angelo, angel hair is a very fine, delicate pasta sold in small, circular nests; its cooking time is minimal because of its extremely thin texture.

seared tuna with kipfler smash and salsa verde

1kg kipfler potatoes, halved
30g butter
1 tablespoon olive oil
4 x 175g tuna steaks
80g baby rocket leaves

salsa verde

½ cup firmly packed fresh
  flat-leaf parsley leaves
¼ cup firmly packed fresh
  mint leaves
⅔ cup (160ml) extra virgin
  olive oil
¼ cup (50g) rinsed, drained
  capers
2 teaspoons dijon mustard
2 tablespoons lemon juice
8 anchovy fillets, drained
1 clove garlic, quartered

1 Boil, steam or microwave potato until tender; drain. Using potato masher, crush potato roughly in large bowl with butter and oil. Cover to keep warm.

2 Meanwhile, make salsa verde.

3 Cook fish on heated oiled grill plate (or grill or barbecue) until browned both sides and cooked as desired.

4 Divide rocket and potato among serving plates; top with fish, drizzle with salsa verde.

salsa verde Blend or process ingredients until just combined. Transfer to medium jug; whisk before pouring over fish.

preparation time 25 minutes
cooking time 20 minutes
serves 4
nutritional count per serving 58.3g total fat; (14g saturated fat); 3695kJ (884 cal); 35.1g carbohydrate; 35g protein; 5.3g fibre
notes If the kipfler potatoes are young and quite small, scrubbing them well, rather than peeling, will be sufficient.
Tuna is at its best if browned both sides but still fairly rare in the middle; overcooking will make it dry.

thai-style green mango salad with seared tuna

1 green mango (350g)
2 teaspoons sesame oil
800g tuna steaks, cut into
    3cm pieces
½ teaspoon dried chilli flakes
2 tablespoons toasted
    sesame seeds
2 cups (100g) snow pea sprouts
½ cup firmly packed fresh
    coriander leaves
½ cup firmly packed fresh
    mint leaves
½ small red onion (50g),
    sliced thinly
lime and ginger dressing
¼ cup (60ml) lime juice
3cm piece fresh ginger (15g),
    grated
1 tablespoon fish sauce

1 Make lime and ginger dressing.
2 Using vegetable peeler, slice mango into thin ribbons.
3 Combine oil and fish in medium bowl. Cook fish on heated oiled grill plate (or grill or barbecue) until cooked as desired.
4 Return fish to same cleaned bowl with chilli and seeds; toss gently.
5 Combine remaining ingredients and dressing in medium bowl. Serve salad topped with fish.
lime and ginger dressing Combine ingredients in screw-top jar; shake well.

preparation time 20 minutes
cooking time 10 minutes
serves 4
nutritional count per serving 17.8g total fat (5.4g saturated fat); 1894kJ (453 cal); 15.5g carbohydrate; 55.5g protein; 3.7g fibre
note Sour and crunchy, green mangoes are just immature fruit. They are available from Asian grocery stores and some greengrocers.

smoked trout, peach and watercress salad

600g piece hot-smoked
  ocean trout
200g watercress, trimmed
2 medium peaches (300g),
  cut into thin wedges
lemon buttermilk dressing
¼ cup (60ml) buttermilk
1 tablespoon lemon juice
1 teaspoon finely grated
  lemon rind
1 teaspoon white sugar

1 Make lemon buttermilk dressing.
2 Discard skin and bones from fish; break
fish into large pieces in medium bowl. Add
watercress and peach; toss gently. Serve
salad drizzled with dressing.
lemon buttermilk dressing Combine
ingredients in screw-top jar; shake well.

preparation time 10 minutes
serves 4
nutritional count per serving 8.1g total fat
(2g saturated fat); 1170kJ (280 cal);
8.7g carbohydrate; 40.7g protein; 3.3g fibre
note Hot-smoked ocean trout can be found,
cryovac-packed, in the refrigerated section of
supermarkets and at fish shops.

grilled fish with roasted corn and chilli salad

4 x 200g white fish steaks

mayonnaise

1 egg yolk

1 clove garlic, crushed

2 tablespoons lime juice

1 teaspoon dijon mustard

¾ cup (180ml) olive oil

corn and chilli salad

8 trimmed corn cobs (2kg)

1 medium red onion (170g),
    chopped finely

2 fresh small red thai chillies,
    chopped finely

⅓ cup coarsely chopped
    fresh coriander

1 Make mayonnaise. Make corn and chilli salad.

2 Cook fish on heated oiled grill plate (or grill or barbecue) until browned both sides and cooked through. Divide corn salad among serving plates; top with fish, drizzle with remaining mayonnaise.

mayonnaise Process egg yolk, garlic, juice and mustard until smooth. With motor operating, gradually add oil in a thin, steady stream; process until mayonnaise thickens slightly.

corn and chilli salad Cook corn on heated oiled grill plate (or grill or barbecue) until browned lightly and just tender. Using sharp knife, remove kernels from cobs. Place kernels in large bowl with onion, chilli, coriander and half the mayonnaise; toss gently to combine.

preparation time 30 minutes
cooking time 25 minutes
serves 4
nutritional count per serving 50.3g total fat;
(7.7g saturated fat); 4038kJ (966 cal);
62.6g carbohydrate; 57.6g protein; 17.3g fibre
note We used mahi mahi in this recipe, but you could also use swordfish or red emperor.

char-grilled fish with roasted mediterranean vegetables

1 medium red capsicum
  (200g), sliced thickly
1 medium yellow capsicum
  (200g), sliced thickly
1 medium eggplant (300g),
  sliced thickly
2 large zucchini (300g),
  sliced thickly
½ cup (125ml) olive oil
250g cherry tomatoes
¼ cup (60ml) balsamic vinegar
1 clove garlic, crushed
2 teaspoons white sugar
4 x 220g white fish steaks
¼ cup coarsely chopped
  fresh basil

1 Preheat oven to 220°/200°C fan-forced.
2 Combine capsicums, eggplant and zucchini with 2 tablespoons of the oil in large baking dish; roast, uncovered, 15 minutes. Add tomatoes; roast, uncovered, about 5 minutes or until vegetables are just tender.
3 Meanwhile, combine remaining oil, vinegar, garlic and sugar in screw-top jar; shake well. Brush a third of the dressing over fish (see note); cook fish, in batches, on heated oiled grill plate (or grill or barbecue) until browned both sides and cooked through.
4 Combine vegetables in large bowl with basil and remaining dressing; toss gently to combine. Divide vegetables among serving plates; top with fish.

preparation time 20 minutes
cooking time 25 minutes
serves 4
nutritional count per serving 33.9g total fat; (5.6g saturated fat); 2270kJ (543 cal); 9.3g carbohydrate; 48.2g protein; 4.8g fibre
notes Don't re-dip the brush used to coat the raw fish into the remaining dressing; if you like, transfer the dressing to coat the fish into a small dish before brushing over the fish. We used swordfish in this recipe, but you could also use mahi mahi or red emperor.

char-grilled fish and vegetables with chilli basil sauce

4 baby cauliflowers (500g), halved
2 trimmed corn cobs (500g), cut into 2cm rounds
400g baby carrots, trimmed
2 tablespoons olive oil
4 x 240g whole white fish
chilli basil sauce
80g butter
2 fresh small red thai chillies, chopped finely
⅓ cup firmly packed fresh basil leaves, shredded finely
1 tablespoon lemon juice

1 Place vegetables and half the oil in large bowl; toss to combine. Cook vegetables on heated oiled grill plate (or grill or barbecue) about 20 minutes or until browned all over and cooked through.

2 Meanwhile, make chilli basil sauce.

3 Score each fish three times both sides; brush all over with remaining oil. Cook fish on heated oiled grill plate (or grill or barbecue) about 5 minutes each side or until cooked through. Serve fish and vegetables drizzled with sauce.

chilli basil sauce Melt butter in small saucepan; add chilli, basil and juice, stir until combined.

preparation time 20 minutes
cooking time 30 minutes
serves 4
nutritional count per serving 32.2g total fat; (13.9g saturated fat); 2608kJ (624 cal); 22.7g carbohydrate; 56.4g protein; 9.3g fibre
note We used whole bream in this recipe, but you could also use whole snapper.

fish cutlets
with mango salsa

4 x 200g white fish cutlets
2 tablespoons lime juice
1 tablespoon fish sauce
1 tablespoon peanut oil
1 tablespoon grated palm sugar
1 teaspoon sambal oelek
2 kaffir lime leaves, shredded finely
mango salsa
2 large mangoes (1.2kg), chopped coarsely
2 lebanese cucumbers (260g), seeded, chopped coarsely
1 fresh long red chilli, sliced thinly
½ cup finely chopped fresh mint

1   Make mango salsa.
2   Cook fish, in batches, on heated oiled grill plate (or grill or barbecue)
until browned both sides and cooked as desired.
3   Place remaining ingredients in screw-top jar; shake well. Divide salsa
and fish among serving plates; drizzle with dressing.
mango salsa   Place ingredients in medium bowl; toss gently to combine.

preparation time 25 minutes
cooking time 15 minutes
serves 4
nutritional count per serving   8.7g total fat; (2g saturated fat);
1501kJ (359 cal); 31.8g carbohydrate; 35.7g protein; 4.3g fibre
note   We used blue-eye cutlets in this recipe, but you could use
any type of fish cutlet.

grilled fish fillets with fennel and onion salad

1 medium red onion (170g), sliced thinly
4 green onions, sliced thinly
1 large fennel bulb (550g), trimmed, sliced thinly
2 stalks celery (300g), trimmed, sliced thinly
½ cup coarsely chopped fresh flat-leaf parsley
⅓ cup (80ml) orange juice
¼ cup (60ml) olive oil
2 cloves garlic, crushed
2 teaspoons sambal oelek
4 x 275g white fish fillets, skin on

1 Combine onions, fennel, celery and parsley in medium bowl.
2 Place juice, oil, garlic and sambal in screw-top jar; shake well.
3 Cook fish on heated oiled grill plate (or grill or barbecue) until browned both sides and cooked as desired.
4 Pour half the dressing over salad in bowl; toss gently to combine. Serve salad topped with fish; drizzle with remaining dressing.

preparation time 15 minutes
cooking time 10 minutes
serves 4
nutritional count per serving 20g total fat; (3.9g saturated fat); 1898kJ (454 cal); 8g carbohydrate; 58.3g protein; 4.5g fibre
note We used snapper fillets in this recipe, but you could use any type of firm white fish fillets.

char-grilled chilli squid and rice noodle salad

800g cleaned squid hoods
450g fresh wide rice noodles
1 medium red capsicum
  (200g), sliced thinly
150g snow peas, trimmed,
  halved
1 lebanese cucumber (130g),
  seeded, sliced thinly
1 small red onion (100g),
  sliced thinly
1 cup loosely packed fresh
  coriander leaves
⅓ cup fresh mint leaves
sweet chilli dressing
½ cup (125ml) water
⅓ cup (75g) caster sugar
1 tablespoon white vinegar
2 fresh small red thai chillies,
  chopped finely

1 Cut squid down centre to open out; score inside in a diagonal pattern. Halve squid lengthways; cut into 3cm pieces.

2 Make sweet chilli dressing.

3 Cook squid on heated oiled grill plate (or grill or barbecue), in batches, until tender and browned lightly.

4 Place noodles in large heatproof bowl, cover with boiling water; separate with fork, drain. Combine noodles in large serving bowl with squid, dressing and remaining ingredients.

sweet chilli dressing Stir the water and sugar in small saucepan, over low heat, until sugar dissolves; bring to the boil. Reduce heat; simmer, uncovered, without stirring, about 5 minutes or until syrup thickens slightly. Stir in vinegar and chilli off the heat.

preparation time 15 minutes
cooking time 15 minutes
serves 4
nutritional count per serving 3.1g total fat (0.8g saturated fat); 1584kJ (379 cal); 48.3g carbohydrate; 38.1g protein; 2.8g fibre

squid salad with garlic lime dressing

1kg cleaned squid hoods
1 fresh long red chilli, chopped finely
1 tablespoon peanut oil
500g rocket, trimmed
150g snow peas, sliced thinly
227g can rinsed, drained water chestnuts, sliced thinly
½ cup loosely packed fresh coriander leaves
½ cup loosely packed fresh mint leaves
garlic lime dressing
¼ cup (60ml) lime juice
2 cloves garlic, crushed
2 tablespoons fish sauce
2 tablespoons grated palm sugar
2 green onions, sliced thinly
1 fresh long red chilli, chopped finely
1 tablespoon peanut oil

1   Make garlic lime dressing.
2   Cut squid down centre to open out; score inside in diagonal pattern then cut into thick strips.
3   Combine squid, chilli and oil in medium bowl. Combine remaining ingredients in large bowl.
4   Cook squid, in batches, on heated oiled grill plate (or grill or barbecue), until tender and browned lightly; combine in bowl with salad and dressing.
garlic lime dressing   Combine ingredients in screw-top jar; shake well.

preparation time 25 minutes
cooking time 20 minutes
serves 4
nutritional count per serving 11.8g total fat (2.1g saturated fat); 1133kJ (271 cal); 15.3g carbohydrate; 23.9g protein; 4.6g fibre

char-grilled octopus salad

1 fresh long red chilli,
  chopped finely
1 teaspoon finely grated
  lime rind
1 teaspoon salt
2 tablespoons rice flour
1kg cleaned octopus,
  quartered
200g mizuna
150g snow peas, sliced thinly
chilli lime dressing
1 fresh small red thai chilli,
  chopped finely
1 teaspoon finely grated
  lime rind
2 tablespoons lime juice
1 tablespoon peanut oil
2cm piece fresh ginger (10g),
  grated

1 Combine chilli, rind, salt and flour in large
bowl; add octopus, toss to coat in mixture.
2 Make chilli lime dressing.
3 Cook octopus on heated oiled grill plate
(or grill or barbecue), in batches, about
20 minutes or until tender.
4 Combine mizuna and snow peas in large
bowl with octopus and dressing.
chilli lime dressing Combine ingredients
in screw-top jar; shake well.

preparation time 20 minutes
cooking time 20 minutes
serves 4
nutritional count per serving 9.4g total fat
(1.8g saturated fat); 1668kJ (399 cal);
10.5g carbohydrate; 65.8g protein; 2.2g fibre

spicy sardines with orange and olive salad

24 butterflied sardines (1kg)
1 clove garlic, crushed
1 tablespoon olive oil
2 tablespoons orange juice
1 teaspoon hot paprika
1 teaspoon finely chopped
   fresh oregano
orange and olive salad
2 medium oranges (480g)
⅓ cup (40g) seeded black
   olives, chopped coarsely
50g baby rocket leaves
1 fresh long red chilli,
   sliced thinly
1 tablespoon orange juice
½ teaspoon finely chopped
   fresh oregano
1 tablespoon olive oil

1 Combine ingredients in medium bowl;
mix gently.
2 Make orange and olive salad.
3 Cook sardines, in batches, on heated
oiled grill plate (or grill or barbecue) until
browned both sides and cooked through.
4 Divide sardines among plates; serve
with salad.
orange and olive salad Peel then segment
oranges over medium bowl; add remaining
ingredients, toss gently to combine.

preparation time 20 minutes
cooking time 15 minutes
serves 4
nutritional count per serving 36.2g total fat
(8.3g saturated fat); 2500kJ (598 cal);
11.5g carbohydrate; 56g protein; 2.2g fibre
note Sardines are available already butterflied
from most fish markets.

thai fish burger

500g firm white fish fillets,
   chopped coarsely
1 tablespoon fish sauce
1 tablespoon kecap manis
1 clove garlic, quartered
1 fresh small red thai chilli,
   chopped coarsely
50g green beans, trimmed,
   chopped coarsely
¼ cup (20g) fried shallots
¼ cup coarsely chopped
   fresh coriander
60g baby spinach leaves
1 lebanese cucumber (130g),
   seeded, sliced thinly
1 tablespoon lime juice
2 teaspoons brown sugar
2 teaspoons fish sauce, extra
4 hamburger buns (360g)
⅓ cup (80ml) sweet chilli sauce

1 Blend or process fish, sauce, kecap manis, garlic and chilli until smooth. Combine fish mixture in large bowl with beans, shallot and coriander; shape into four patties.
2 Cook patties on heated oiled flat plate about 15 minutes or until cooked.
3 Toss spinach, cucumber and combined juice, sugar and extra sauce in medium bowl.
4 Split buns in half; toast cut sides. Sandwich salad, patties and sweet chilli sauce bun halves.

preparation time 20 minutes
cooking time 15 minutes
serves 4
nutritional count per serving 5.3g total fat (0.7g saturated fat); 1722kJ (412 cal); 55.2g carbohydrate; 32g protein; 5.7g fibre
notes We used blue-eye in this recipe, but any firm white fish fillets can be used.
Fried shallots are available from Asian grocery stores; they'll keep for months if stored tightly sealed. You can make your own by frying thinly sliced shallots until golden.

fish with tomato, caper and walnut dressing

4 x 185g white fish fillets
tomato, caper and walnut dressing
250g cherry tomatoes
60g butter
1 tablespoon finely grated lemon rind
2 teaspoons lemon juice
1 teaspoon rinsed, drained capers, chopped finely
¼ cup (30g) finely chopped walnuts
½ cup coarsely chopped fresh flat-leaf parsley

1 Make tomato, caper and walnut dressing.
2 Cook fish on oiled grill plate (or grill or barbecue). Serve with dressing.
tomato, caper and walnut dressing Cook tomatoes on heated, oiled grill plate until tender. Melt butter in small saucepan; add tomatoes and remaining ingredients, stir until hot.

preparation time 15 minutes
cooking time 20 minutes
serves 4
nutritional count per serving 19.8g total fat (9.2g saturated fat); 1471kJ (352 cal); 2g carbohydrate; 40.1g protein; 1.9g fibre
note We used barramundi fish fillets in this recipe, but you could use any firm white fish fillets.

fish with chunky tomato, anchovy and caper sauce

1 tablespoon olive oil
4 x 200g white fish fillets
1 medium brown onion (150g), chopped finely
2 cloves garlic, crushed
4 medium tomatoes (600g), peeled, seeded, chopped coarsely
4 anchovy fillets, drained, chopped finely
1 tablespoon rinsed, drained capers
1 teaspoon white sugar
¼ cup coarsely chopped fresh flat-leaf parsley

1   Heat half the oil in large frying pan; cook fish, uncovered, until cooked through.
2   Meanwhile, heat remaining oil in small saucepan; cook onion and garlic, stirring, until onion softens. Add tomato; cook, stirring, 1 minute. Remove from heat; stir in anchovy, capers, sugar and parsley. Serve fish with sauce, and lemon wedges, if desired.

preparation time 15 minutes
cooking time 15 minutes
serves 4
nutritional count per serving   7.1g total fat (1.1g saturated fat); 1099kJ (263 cal); 6.4g carbohydrate; 41.8g protein; 2.8g fibre
note   We used blue-eye fillets in this recipe, but you can use any firm white fish fillets.

steamed fish with chilli and ginger

2 baby buk choy (300g), quartered lengthways
2 x 200g white fish cutlets
10cm piece fresh ginger (50g), cut into long strips
2 green onions, cut into long strips
¼ cup (60ml) light soy sauce
1 teaspoon sesame oil
1 fresh long red chilli, sliced thinly
1 cup loosely packed fresh coriander leaves

1 Place buk choy on large heatproof plate inside bamboo steamer; top with fish. Sprinkle ginger and onion over fish; drizzle with sauce and oil.
2 Steam fish, covered, over wok of simmering water, about 5 minutes or until cooked through. Serve fish topped with chilli and coriander.

preparation time 10 minutes
cooking time 10 minutes
serves 4
nutritional count per serving 3.9g total fat (1.1g saturated fat); 786kJ (188 cal); 2.3g carbohydrate; 347g protein; 1.8g fibre
note We used snapper cutlets in this recipe, but you could use any white fish cutlets.

seafood ravioli
with sesame dressing

250g uncooked medium
   king prawns
100g firm white fish fillets,
   chopped coarsely
2 cloves garlic, crushed
2cm piece fresh ginger (10g),
   grated
½ teaspoon sesame oil
24 wonton wrappers
12 scallops without roe (300g)
1 egg white, beaten lightly
½ cup loosely packed fresh
   coriander leaves
2 green onions, sliced thinly
sesame dressing
2 tablespoons kecap manis
2 tablespoons
   rice wine vinegar
¼ teaspoon sesame oil
1 fresh long red chilli,
   sliced thinly

1 Shell and devein prawns; chop prawn meat coarsely. Blend or process prawn, fish, garlic, ginger and oil until mixture forms a coarse paste.
2 Place one heaped teaspoon of prawn mixture in centre of each of 12 wrappers; top each with a scallop. Brush edges of wrappers with egg white; top each with another wrapper, pressing edges together firmly.
3 Using the blunt edge of 5.5cm round cutter, gently press down around filling to enclose securely. Using 7cm cutter, cut filled ravioli into rounds; discard excess wonton wrapper. Rest ravioli on a tea-towel-lined tray
4 Make sesame dressing.
5 Cook ravioli, uncovered, in two batches, in large saucepan of gently boiling water, about 3 minutes or until ravioli float to the surface. Remove from pan; drain on absorbent paper.
6 Divide ravioli among serving plates; drizzle with dressing, sprinkle with coriander and onion.
sesame dressing Combine ingredients in screw-top jar; shake well.

preparation time 30 minutes
cooking time 10 minutes
serves 4
nutritional count per serving 2.8g total fat (0.6g saturated fat); 614kJ (147 cal); 2.7g carbohydrate; 27.2g protein; 0.6g fibre

thai-style seafood vermicelli

125g bean thread vermicelli

700g uncooked medium
king prawns

1 litre (4 cups) water

3cm piece fresh ginger (15g),
sliced thinly

10cm stick fresh lemon grass
(20g), chopped coarsely

2 cloves garlic, sliced thinly

440g salmon fillets

150g snow peas, trimmed,
sliced thinly

8 red radishes (280g),
trimmed, sliced thinly

½ cup coarsely chopped
fresh coriander

3 green onions, sliced thickly

sweet chilli dressing

2 tablespoons fish sauce

2 tablespoons sweet chilli sauce

⅓ cup (80ml) lime juice

1 fresh long red chilli,
chopped finely

1 tablespoon grated
palm sugar

1 Place vermicelli in large heatproof bowl, cover with boiling water; stand until just tender, drain. Rinse under cold water; drain.

2 Shell and devein prawns.

3 Place the water, ginger, lemon grass and garlic in medium frying pan; bring to the boil. Add seafood; reduce heat. Cook, covered, until prawns are changed in colour and fish is cooked as desired; drain. Cool fish slightly; flake into chunks.

4 Meanwhile, make sweet chilli dressing.

5 Combine vermicelli, seafood, dressing and remaining ingredients in large bowl.

sweet chilli dressing Combine ingredients in screw-top jar; shake well.

preparation time 15 minutes
cooking time 15 minutes
serves 4
nutritional count per serving 8.7g total fat (1.8g saturated fat); 1584kJ (379 cal); 30.3g carbohydrate; 44.5g protein; 3.5g fibre

kung pao prawns

Kung pao, a classic Sichuan stir-fry, is made with either seafood or chicken, peanuts and lots of chillies. An authentic Sichuan-Chinese restaurant always has a delicious kung pao.

28 uncooked large king prawns (2kg)
2 tablespoons peanut oil
2 cloves garlic, crushed
4 fresh small red thai chillies, chopped finely
1 teaspoon sichuan peppercorns, crushed
500g choy sum, trimmed, chopped coarsely
¼ cup (60ml) light soy sauce
¼ cup (60ml) chinese cooking wine
1 teaspoon white sugar
227g can rinsed, drained water chestnuts, halved
4 green onions, chopped coarsely
½ cup (70g) roasted unsalted peanuts

1   Shell and devein prawns, leaving tails intact.
2   Heat half the oil in wok; stir-fry prawns, in batches, until changed in colour. Drain.
3   Heat remaining oil in wok; stir-fry garlic, chilli and peppercorns until fragrant. Add choy sum; stir-fry until wilted.
4   Return prawns to wok with sauce, wine, sugar and chestnuts; stir-fry 2 minutes. Remove from heat; stir in onion and nuts.

preparation time 30 minutes
cooking time 15 minutes
serves 4
nutritional count per serving 19.4g total fat (2.9g saturated fat); 1998kJ (478 cal); 8.5g carbohydrate; 8.5g protein; 7.5g fibre

barbecued prawns
with chilli lime dressing

1.7kg uncooked large king prawns

¼ cup coarsely chopped fresh coriander

chilli lime dressing

⅓ cup (80ml) lime juice

⅓ cup (80ml) lemon juice

½ cup (125ml) olive oil

2 cloves garlic, crushed

2 teaspoons caster sugar

2 teaspoons sea salt flakes

3 fresh long red chillies, sliced thinly

1 Make chilli lime dressing.

2 Using small sharp knife, devein prawns, leaving heads and shells intact. Combine prawns in large bowl with half the dressing; cook prawns on heated oiled grill plate (or grill or barbecue) until cooked through.

3 Stir coriander into remaining dressing; serve with prawns.

chilli lime dressing Combine ingredients in small bowl.

preparation time 30 minutes

cooking time 5 minutes

serves 4

nutritional count per serving 29.8g total fat (4.2g saturated fat); 1914kJ (458 cal); 3.4g carbohydrate; 44.1g protein; 0.4g fibre

prawn and scallop chilli jam stir-fry

1kg uncooked medium king prawns
2 tablespoons peanut oil
300g scallops, roe removed
2 cloves garlic, crushed
2cm piece fresh ginger (10g), grated
200g green beans, cut into 5cm lengths
350g gai lan, trimmed, chopped coarsely
⅔ cup (220g) thai chilli jam
1½ cups (120g) bean sprouts
½ cup firmly packed thai basil leaves

1   Shell and devein prawns leaving tails intact.
2   Heat half the oil in wok; stir-fry prawns and scallops, in batches, until cooked as desired. Drain on absorbent paper.
3   Heat remaining oil in wok; stir-fry garlic and ginger until fragrant. Add beans and gai lan; stir-fry until gai lan is wilted. Return prawns and scallops to wok with chilli jam; stir-fry 2 minutes.
4   Stir in sprouts and basil off the heat; serve with steamed jasmine rice, if desired.

preparation time 20 minutes
cooking time 20 minutes
serves 4
nutritional count per serving 14.6g total fat (2.9g saturated fat); 1513kJ (362 cal); 16.8g carbohydrate; 38.6g protein; 3.9g fibre
note Thai chilli jam is available from Asian food shops and some major supermarkets.

chilli prawn
and lime risotto

10cm stick fresh lemon grass (20g), halved lengthways
1 litre (4 cups) chicken stock
1½ cups (375ml) water
1 tablespoon finely grated lime rind
½ cup (125ml) lime juice
30g butter
2 cloves garlic, crushed
2 fresh small red thai chillies, chopped finely
2 cups (400g) arborio rice
1kg uncooked medium king prawns
⅓ cup fresh mint leaves

1 Bruise lemon grass; combine in medium saucepan with stock, the water, rind and juice. Bring to the boil; reduce heat, simmer, covered.
2 Melt butter in large saucepan; cook garlic and chilli, stirring, until fragrant. Add rice; stir to coat in butter mixture. Add 1 cup simmering stock mixture; cook, stirring, over low heat, until stock is absorbed. Continue adding stock mixture, in 1 cup batches, stirring, until absorbed between additions. Total cooking time should be about 25 minutes or until rice is just tender.
3 Meanwhile, shell and devein prawns, leaving tails intact. Discard lemon grass from risotto, add prawns; cook, stirring gently, until prawns are changed in colour. Stir in mint off the heat.

preparation time 10 minutes
cooking time 35 minutes
serves 4
nutritional count per serving 8.6g total fat (4.8g saturated fat); 2366kJ (566 cal); 83.7g carbohydrate; 35.7g protein; 1.5g fibre

glossary

aborio rice small, round grain rice, well-suited to absorb a large amount of liquid; especially suitable for risottos.

basil, thai also known as horapa. Has smallish leaves and a sweet licorice/aniseed taste. Available in Asian grocery stores and some major supermarkets.

buk choy also known as bok choy, pak choi, chinese white cabbage or chinese chard; has a fresh, mild mustard taste. Baby buk choy, also known as pak kat farang or shanghai bok choy, is much smaller and more tender.

capers the grey-green buds of a warm climate (usually Mediterranean) shrub, sold either dried and salted or pickled in a vinegar brine. Rinse well before using.

chilli use rubber gloves when seeding and chopping fresh chillies as they can burn your skin. Removing seeds and membranes lessens the heat level.

chinese cooking wine also known as hao hsing or chinese rice wine; mirin or sherry can be substituted.

choy sum also known as pakaukeo or flowering cabbage; has long stems, light green leaves and yellow flowers. Stems and leaves are both edible, steamed or stir-fried.

ciabatta in Italian, the word means slipper, the traditional shape of this popular crisp-crusted, open-textured white sourdough bread.

coriander also known as cilantro or chinese parsley; bright-green leafy herb with a pungent flavour. The stems and roots of coriander are also used; wash well before chopping finely.

gai lan also known as gai larn, gai lum, chinese broccoli and chinese kale; prized more for its stems than its coarse leaves.

ginger also known as green or root ginger; the thick root of a tropical plant.

green mango sour and crunchy, these are just immature fruit that can be eaten as a vegetable.

haloumi cheese a firm, cream-coloured sheep-milk cheese matured in brine; somewhat like a minty, salty fetta in flavour. Should be eaten while still warm as it becomes tough and rubbery on cooling.

kaffir lime leaves also known as bai magrood; looks like two glossy dark green leaves joined end to end, forming a rounded hourglass shape. Dried leaves are less potent, so double the number if you substitute them for fresh leaves. A strip of fresh lime peel may be substituted for each kaffir lime leaf.

kecap manis also known as ketjap manis; a thick soy sauce with added sugar and spices.

kipfler potatoes small, finger-shaped potatoes with a nutty flavour.

lebanese cucumber short, slender and thin-skinned. Probably the most popular variety because of its tender, edible skin, tiny, yielding seeds and sweet, fresh and flavoursome taste.

lemon grass a tall, clumping, lemon-smelling and -tasting, sharp-edged grass; the white lower part of each stem is chopped and used.

mizuna japanese in origin; frizzy green salad leaves with a delicate mustard flavour.

noodles

  bean thread also known as wun sen, cellophane or glass noodles. Made from mung bean paste. White in colour (not off-white like rice vermicelli), very delicate and fine; available dried in various-sized bundles. Must be soaked to soften before use; using them deep-fried requires no pre-soaking.

  fresh rice also known as ho fun, khao pun, sen yau, pho or kway tiau. Purchase in strands of various widths or large sheets weighing about 500g, which are cut into the noodle-size desired. Chewy and pure white, they do not need pre-cooking before use.

onions

green also known as scallion or, incorrectly, shallot; an immature onion picked before the bulb has formed, having a long, bright-green edible stalk.

shallots also called french shallots, golden shallots or eschalots; small, brown-skinned, elongated members of the onion family.

palm sugar also known as nam tan pip, jaggery, jawa or gula melaka; made from the sap of the sugar palm tree. Light brown to black in colour and usually sold in rock-hard cakes. Brown sugar can be substituted if palm sugar is unavailable.

paprika ground dried sweet red capsicum (bell pepper).

parsley, flat-leaf also known as continental parsley or italian parsley.

rocket also known as rugula, arugula and rucola.

sambal oelek (also ulek or olek) Indonesian in origin; a salty paste made from ground chillies and vinegar.

sauce

fish also called nam pla or nuoc nam; made from pulverised salted fermented fish, most often anchovies. Has a pungent smell and strong taste; use sparingly.

soy made from fermented soy beans. Several variations are available in Asian food stores and supermarkets.

light soy a fairly thin, pale salty sauce; used in dishes in which the natural colour of the ingredients is to be maintained. Not to be confused with salt-reduced or low-sodium soy sauces.

sweet chilli a mild, thai-style sauce made from red chillies, sugar, garlic and vinegar.

scallops a bivalve mollusc with a fluted shell valve; we use scallops that have the coral (roe) attached.

sichuan peppercorns also known as szechuan or chinese pepper; native to the Sichuan province of China. A mildly-hot spice; although it is not related to the peppercorn family, its small, red-brown aromatic sichuan berries look like black peppercorns and have a distinctive peppery-lemon flavour and aroma.

spinach also known as english spinach and incorrectly, silver beet.

thai chilli jam a sweet, sourish tangy jam that is sold in jars at supermarkets and Asian grocery stores. Refrigerate after opening.

vinegar

balsamic made from the juice of Trebbiano grapes; it is a deep rich brown colour with a sweet and sour flavour. Quality can be determined up to a point by price; use the most expensive sparingly.

cider (apple cider) made from fermented apples.

rice wine made from rice wine lees (sediment left after fermentation), salt and alcohol.

white made from spirit of cane sugar.

wasabi an Asian horseradish sold in powdered or paste form. Used to make the pungent, green-coloured sauce traditionally served with Japanese raw fish.

water chestnuts small brown tubers with a crisp, white, nutty-tasting flesh. Their crunchy texture is best experienced fresh; however, canned water chestnuts are more easily obtained and can be kept for about a month in the fridge once opened.

watercress also known as winter rocket. One of the cress family, a large group of peppery greens. Highly perishable, so must be used as soon as possible after purchase.

white fish fillets any firm, boneless white fish fillet – blue eye, bream, swordfish, ling, whiting or sea perch are all good choices. Check for any small bones in the fillets and use tweezers to remove them.

wonton wrappers also known as wonton skins; gow gee, egg or spring roll pastry sheets can be substituted.

conversion chart

MEASURES

One Australian metric measuring cup holds approximately 250ml, one Australian metric tablespoon holds 20ml, one Australian metric teaspoon holds 5ml.

The difference between one country's measuring cups and another's is within a 2- or 3-teaspoon variance, and will not affect your cooking results. North America, New Zealand and the United Kingdom use a 15ml tablespoon. All cup and spoon measurements are level. The most accurate way of measuring dry ingredients is to weigh them. When measuring liquids, use a clear glass or plastic jug with metric markings.

We use large eggs with an average weight of 60g.

DRY MEASURES

METRIC	IMPERIAL
15g	½oz
30g	1oz
60g	2oz
90g	3oz
125g	4oz (¼lb)
155g	5oz
185g	6oz
220g	7oz
250g	8oz (½lb)
280g	9oz
315g	10oz
345g	11oz
375g	12oz (¾lb)
410g	13oz
440g	14oz
470g	15oz
500g	16oz (1lb)
750g	24oz (1½lb)
1kg	32oz (2lb)

LIQUID MEASURES

METRIC	IMPERIAL
30ml	1 fluid oz
60ml	2 fluid oz
100ml	3 fluid oz
125ml	4 fluid oz
150ml	5 fluid oz (¼ pint/1 gill)
190ml	6 fluid oz
250ml	8 fluid oz
300ml	10 fluid oz (½ pint)
500ml	16 fluid oz
600ml	20 fluid oz (1 pint)
1000ml (1 litre)	1¾ pints

LENGTH MEASURES

METRIC	IMPERIAL
3mm	⅛in
6mm	¼in
1cm	½in
2cm	¾in
2.5cm	1in
5cm	2in
6cm	2½in
8cm	3in
10cm	4in
13cm	5in
15cm	6in
18cm	7in
20cm	8in
23cm	9in
25cm	10in
28cm	11in
30cm	12in (1ft)

OVEN TEMPERATURES

These oven temperatures are only a guide for conventional ovens.
For fan-forced ovens, check the manufacturer's manual.

	°C (CELSIUS)	°F (FAHRENHEIT)	GAS MARK
Very slow	120	250	½
Slow	150	275-300	1-2
Moderately slow	160	325	3
Moderate	180	350-375	4-5
Moderately hot	200	400	6
Hot	220	425-450	7-8
Very hot	240	475	9

index

If you like this cookbook, you'll love these...

These are just a small selection of titles available in *The Australian Women's Weekly* range
on sale at selected newsagents and supermarkets or online at www.acpbooks.com.au